My Monthly Journal

With Inspirational Bible Verses to Start Each Day

Vision Spots Publishing

Copyright Notice

Introduction

This is your daily journal for the next 31 days. Each day's journal entry begins with a Bible verse followed by your journal pages waiting to capture your thoughts, experiences, inspirations, & blessings.

Purpose yourself to complete one journal each month for the next twelve months. Then....go back and read what you captured. Look at what you learned, bear witness to how God has blessed you, and see how He used the good, the bad, and the "old you" for His glory.

NAME: _____

MONTH: _____

Day 1

"Forget the former things; Do not dwell on the past. See, I am doing a new thing! Now it springs up; do you not perceive it? I am making a way in the wilderness and streams in the wasteland." — Isaiah 43:18-19, NIV

_____

_____

_____

_____

_____

_____

_____

_____

_____

_____

_____

_____

_____

Day 2

"Trust in the LORD with all your heart, and lean not on your own understanding." – Proverbs 3:5, NKJV

_____

_____

_____

_____

_____

_____

_____

_____

_____

_____

_____

_____

_____

_____

DAY 3

"In all your ways acknowledge Him, and He shall
direct your paths." — Proverbs 3:6, NKJV

_____

_____

_____

_____

_____

_____

_____

_____

_____

_____

_____

_____

_____

_____

_____

_____

_____

Day 4

"I praise you, for I am fearfully and wonderfully made. Wonderful are your works; My soul knows it very well." - Psalm 139:14, ESV

_____

_____

_____

_____

_____

_____

_____

_____

_____

_____

_____

_____

_____

_____

_____

_____

Day 5

"Have I not commanded you? Be strong and courageous. Do not be terrified; do not be discouraged, for the LORD your God will be with you wherever you go." — Joshua 1:9, NIV

_____

_____

_____

_____

_____

_____

_____

_____

_____

_____

_____

_____

_____

_____

_____

Day 6

"Let us not love in word, neither in tongue; but in
deed and in truth." — 1 John 3:18, KJV

_____

_____

_____

_____

_____

_____

_____

_____

_____

_____

_____

_____

_____

_____

_____

_____

_____

Day 7

"Let not your heart be troubled: ye believe in God, believe also in me." — John 14:1, KJV

Day 8

"A joyful heart is good medicine, but a crushed spirit dries up the bones." — Proverbs 17:22 (NIV)

_____

_____

_____

_____

_____

_____

_____

_____

_____

_____

_____

_____

_____

_____

_____

_____

Day 9

"And may you have the power to understand, as all God's people should, how wide, how long, how high, and how deep his love is." — Ephesians 3:18, NLT

_____

_____

_____

_____

_____

_____

_____

_____

_____

_____

_____

_____

_____

_____

Day 10

"And the peace of God, which transcends all understanding, will guard your hearts and your minds in Christ Jesus." – Philippians 4:7, NIV

_____

_____

_____

_____

_____

_____

_____

_____

_____

_____

_____

_____

_____

Day 11

"The Lord directs the steps of the godly. He delights in every detail of their lives. Though they stumble, they will never fall, for the Lord holds them by the hand." – Psalm 37:23-24, NLT

_____

_____

_____

_____

_____

_____

_____

_____

_____

_____

_____

_____

_____

_____

_____

Day 12

"I pray that God, the source of hope, will fill you completely with joy and peace because you trust in him." — Romans 15:13, NLT

Day 13

"Your loving kindness is better than life, My lips
shall praise You, Thus I will bless You while I live;
I will lift up my hands in Your name."

Psalm 63:3-4, NKJV

_____

_____

_____

_____

_____

_____

_____

_____

_____

_____

_____

_____

_____

Day 14

"Those who give to the poor will lack nothing, but those who close their eyes to them receive many curses."– Proverbs 28:27, NIV

_____

_____

_____

_____

_____

_____

_____

_____

_____

_____

_____

_____

_____

_____

Day 15

"A soft answer turns away wrath, but a harsh word stirs up anger." — Proverbs 15:1, ESV

_____

_____

_____

_____

_____

_____

_____

_____

_____

_____

_____

_____

_____

_____

_____

_____

Day 16

"But you are a chosen people, a royal priesthood, a holy nation, God's special possession, that you may declare the praises of him who called you out of darkness into his wonderful light." — 1 Peter 2:9, NIV

_____

_____

_____

_____

_____

_____

_____

_____

_____

_____

_____

_____

_____

_____

Day 17

"He will once again fill your mouth with laughter,
and your lips with shouts of joy." — Job 8:21, NLT

_____

_____

_____

_____

_____

_____

_____

_____

_____

_____

_____

_____

_____

_____

_____

_____

_____

Day 18

"Your word is a lamp to guide my feet, and a light for my path." — Psalm 119:105, NLT

_____

_____

_____

_____

_____

_____

_____

_____

_____

_____

_____

_____

_____

_____

_____

_____

Day 19

"Therefore, if anyone is in Christ, he is a new creation. The old has passed away; behold, the new has come."– 2 Corinthians 5:17, ESV

_____

_____

_____

_____

_____

_____

_____

_____

_____

_____

_____

_____

_____

_____

_____

_____

Day 20

"I will bless the Lord at all times: his praise shall continually be in my mouth." — Psalm 34:34, KJV

_____

_____

_____

_____

_____

_____

_____

_____

_____

_____

_____

_____

_____

_____

_____

_____

Day 21

"Be kind to one another, tender-hearted,
forgiving one another, as God in Christ forgave
you." — Ephesians 4:32, ESV

_____

_____

_____

_____

_____

_____

_____

_____

_____

_____

_____

_____

_____

_____

_____

Day 22

"You made all the delicate, inner parts of my
body, and knit me together in my mother's womb.
Thank you for making me so wonderfully
complex!" — Psalm 139:13-14, NLT

_____

_____

_____

_____

_____

_____

_____

_____

_____

_____

_____

_____

_____

_____

Day 23

"May the words of my mouth and the meditation of my heart be pleasing in Your sight, O Lord, my Rock and my Redeemer." — Psalm 19:14, NIV

_____

_____

_____

_____

_____

_____

_____

_____

_____

_____

_____

_____

_____

_____

_____

Day 24

"But seek first the kingdom of God and his righteousness, and all these things will be added to you." — Matthew 6:33, ESV

Day 25

"Whatever you do, do it heartily, as to the Lord and not to men." — Colossians 3:23, NKJV

Day 26

"Let us therefore make every effort to do what
leads to peace and to mutual edification." —
Romans 14:19, NIV

_____

_____

_____

_____

_____

_____

_____

_____

_____

_____

_____

_____

_____

_____

Day 27

"…That my tongue and my heart and everything glorious within me may sing praise to You and not be silent. O Lord my God, I will give thanks to You forever." – Psalm 106:1, AMP

Day 28

"Commit to the Lord whatever you do, and your plans will succeed." – Proverbs 16:3, NIV

Day 29

"Don't jump to conclusions — there may be a
perfectly good explanation for what you just saw."
— Proverbs 25:8, MSG

Day 30

"My dear brothers and sisters, take note of this:
Everyone should be quick to listen, slow to speak
and slow to become angry." — James 1:19, NIV

_____

_____

_____

_____

_____

_____

_____

_____

_____

_____

_____

_____

_____

_____

Day 31

"O come, let us worship and bow down: let us
kneel before the LORD our maker." — Psalm 95:6,
KJV

_____

_____

_____

_____

_____

_____

_____

_____

_____

_____

_____

_____

_____

Printed in Great Britain
by Amazon